All Rivers

Are One

Paul Bach, Jr.

All photography by author except:

pages 51, 56, 61 and 105 by t.k. splake, used with permission.

Author photo by Sarah Bach.

Poem "Bliss" found in image on page 112 originally saw print in
Portolano, Charles, ed. The Weekly Avocet. No. 15, 2013.

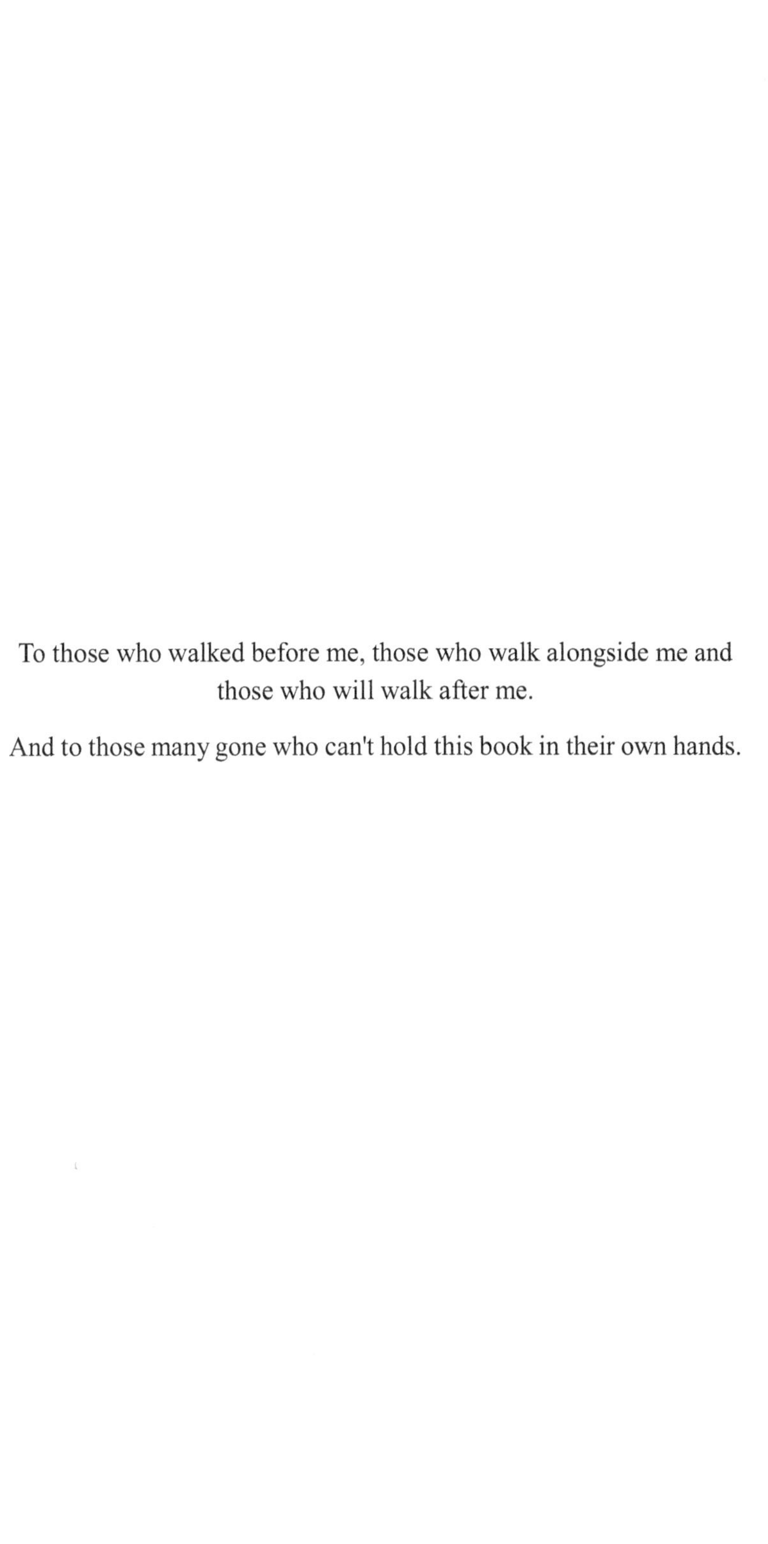

To those who walked before me, those who walk alongside me and those who will walk after me.

And to those many gone who can't hold this book in their own hands.

Contents

po·et·ry

[po-a-tree] *noun*

Form of literature that uses aesthetics and rhythm of language to evoke meanings, sometimes different than the apparent conventional meaning.

As in: the hidden
meaning of things,
said
but not said,
that's what you get from *poetry*.

As in: the moon,
the stars,
your own backyard,
that's where *poetry* can take you.

As in: salvation, of one kind
or another,
save the day
or save
my life,
that's what *poetry* can do for you

Blasphemy

This book, this story
this
poem
contains mature
language

By all means,
yes!
give me
mature language
mature concepts
mature thoughts
mature theories

Let it rain
down
in sheets,
cover the Earth

The next great flood
remake the world entire.

The Blank Page

Beckoning, taunting
demanding, forceful
attack
do battle
wrestle
draw blood, letting truth out
battle-scarred
this page

Easier to
wish
mind blank

Intruder

Squirrels
at play
scamper
and scatter
up
and over
down
and around
the tree

Caring
not at
all
the writer
watching

The Poet Tree

For TKS

This tree
gives its
skin
to the
Poet Tree

As this poet
gives
his blood

To support
the mission
of both the tree
and the man
who tends the
tree

Work the words
and for the benefit of all
disperse
to the four winds.

Travel
Songs

On the Wing

Unimaginable
unnatural
to gaze out upon
the tops of clouds

As if
islands
floating in
misty sea

Thickening to
frozen wasteland

Mirroring
as Artic
Circle beckons

Streets of Beijing

Nothing strikes
so suddenly
as fear
born of
hearing
Police yelling
in a language
you don't
understand

Cold Mountain

After Han Shan

I have never been
to Cold Mountain
yet I carry
Cold Mountain with me

Cold Mountain
in the depths of valleys
Cold Mountain in the
driest heat

Will you come
to Cold Mountain?
Will Cold Mountain
travel with you?

Don't Speak of It

The ghosts of Tiananmen
haunt the living
evident throughout
every action
unspoken, unacknowledged

Precise martial movement
and military announcement
tourist wandering
student demonstration

The camera eye
always
watching

American Guilt

Paranoia

rightly or wrongly

that comes
with hearing
"foreigner" directed
at you
in a jumble of words
you cannot understand

Intent
or interpretation

whose reality?

Tourist

Spreading the dust of
time

Beijing's emperors
to
the Bird's Nest

Archaeology

Dinosaurs
buried
in the earth
dreaming
of flight

become
dragons
merely sleeping

Times
determine
Truth

Flying Home

My time reverses
while yours
proceeds

Distance between us
grows
in space and time

Heart connection
stretched
unbroken

(W)rites of Spring

Traveling miles
North to South
Michigan
top to bottom
reminded why
I am a child
of April, Spring

Renewal, rebirth
resurrection
this
the New Year

All starts
fresh
green from
grey
life from
death

What more
Spring-like
than Easter?

Dead will rise
sun will shine
world in bloom
words from the
page

What better time
to be
(re)born?

61 Highway Sprawls

"...I think it can be very easily done
We'll just put some bleachers out in the sun
And have it out on Highway 61..."

-Bob Dylan, "Highway 61 Revisited"

61 shimmers,
fugitive figures
flicker, focus
and fade,
spectral
in the distance

"I've been to the mountaintop."

Snap brim fedora
floats
dusty road
shifts to four lanes

"...Didn't nobody seem to know me, babe-everybody pass me
by..."

Fragments
of conversations
drift

"The past is never dead, it is not even past."

Always sound,
rhythm
fills the air

"…a combination of the first two letters of Stewart and
Axton…"

Casinos burst
into bloom
gaudy with light
and color

"…shimmered like the wings of a lighted dragonfly…"

 Rising and falling
like waves

"Our first job was to get people out of trees and off of roofs…"

Shifting closer
only to recede
ramshackle structures
take their place

"I wanted the world to see what they did to my baby."

From tragedy to farce,

"When off duty, the ducks live in the Royal Duck Palace on the
hotel's rooftop."

salvation

"…a school in self-government…"

to damnation,

"Sin is the engineer, pleasure is the headlight and the Devil is the
conductor."

Whether earned
or not,
we're all aboard

There's always room
on the Black Diamond Train.

From a wasteland
over a million miles
under an average of
ten feet of water
to culture's
driver

As Mississippi leads,
so follows America

Boy, don't you know the entire delta
is
ground zero?

All That Remains

Upon viewing the remnants of the Gennett Records facility,
Richmond Indiana

Bustling production
vast complex
pianos, phonographs
music first recorded
etched into the grooves

Over time
business lost
Great Depression
forced to close

Complex not maintained
history disregarded
buildings knocked down

One remaining shell
saved before destroyed
sentinel with windows gone

Wind free to
blow in, around
through

Close your eyes
music in the air
again, floating on
the breeze

Listen.

A Simple Wish

For C. H. in the hopes that…

To always hear the soothing
in your voice,

To always feel as if falling
into your deep, brown eyes,

To always yearn to be
closer, even as we touch

To always feel you near
no matter the distance

Will you meet me
in the moonlight?
the sunlight?
the driving rain
and blinding snow?

Will you meet me
over and over
as if we never had?

As our life
is spent
our hearts
close

beating
against each other
faster
and faster?

Impressions of Beauty

(after Midnight, New Year's)

Arm around
her waist,
hand on flat stomach,
pulled close

A smattering of freckles
beneath her eyes

Touching up lipstick red
as blood

Face to face,
knees touching,
heads leaning in,
then touching, resting
against the other, listening

A beginning
with the ending as close

as the space
between us

Nonresponsive

My words scatter
over you
like
breakers

they ebb
and they flow

I have labored, deliberated
bled
and worked these words,
tear-stained,
chosen,
loved and
hated,
bringing pain
and
joy

In the end,
meaning
nothing

Birthday

A single
candle
holding all
the hopes
of so many

When not used,
the heartbreak
never leaves

Echoes

The creak
of the floor
with the weight
of your step

The comfort
of your body
next to mine
asleep or awake

The shift
in the bed
as your body
moves in sleep

The smell
of your perfume
upon smooth, soft skin
still in my head

All echoes,
echoes again.

Form and Function

Thrill of silhouette
heart pounding
at the sight
of you
bare, uncovered

Over time
looking, anticipating
touching
years or months
thoughts of forever

Now
I can't recall how you looked
unclad
shades of color
shape and size

relegated to the past
along with that fool
who thought it'd last

Never Satisfied

Serene
sound of waves
far from silent

colors in bloom
warmth of the sun
content

If only
heartache
erased

sharing
with you
at my
side

Little Flower

Deep eyes
that pull

Touch that
comforts
while
building desire

soothing tones

All is right
with the world

Our embrace.

Moonrise

"A single moonshine in every drop of water
Every water-drop moon, the very same moon."-Yung-chia

Will you look with me at the wonders reflected in the water
whether standing arms clasped, heart to heart
or separated by time and miles

Same moon, same moon

Life
Songs

Beatle Dream

I believe
in Beatle Dream
of peace and
love is all you need

That work,
your job should not
define your life

That there are wonders in the world
if you look
that only get more wondrous
if shared

That Beauty abounds

And most
of all

That the collective
unconscious
tells us
what we all
already know

the meaning of life
is love

The Glue

Negotiations
lies
compromise
going against
your nature

Nothing held
back
truth
polite
impolite

All attempts
at patching,
healing
the rift

When the glue
does not have
time
to set
or
is used
to bind
opposing
materials

Stretched
beyond
its grasp

The glue,
regardless
of intent,
the glue
will not
hold

Occupy

From a voice
for decades
declaiming
CHANGE
is the only answer,
I'm with you

Calmer heads prevail
peaceful gatherings
coast to coast
and rising
nation to nation,
I'm with you

From miles and continents away
yet by your
side,
I'm with you

Ninety-nine is more
than one
and always will be

With a Guy Fawkes mask
in one hand,

I'm with you
With the shade of Thoreau
and a copy of "On Civil Disobedience"

in the other,
I'm with you

"Letter from Birmingham Jail"
MLK, join hands
I'm with you

Readings on site
all over the country
of Ginsberg's "America"
resurrect his spirit,
I'm with you

The creaking of branches
A low rumble is heard
exhaling through the leaves
the voice of Whitman
echoes off the buildings
the trees, the hills

I'm with you

I'm with you...

Mercy?
Do you ask for mercy?

You will be given a toad and
a bucket of salt and nothing
more.

Do not ask for more,
there is none.

...And These Are My Faults

with apologies to Cecilia Woloch

Blazing naivete
the willingness
to take someone
at their word
while always
not trusting
in any system
or government,
structure
and form
imposed,
irrational but true.

Stubborn
(I come by
my demons
naturally)
to the point of
unstoppable force
meet
immovable object
others upset,
Angered
unintentional byproduct

of my actions.

Seeing
in black
and white,
right
and wrong
A is
A
when nothing
is that easy
or clear.

A desire
to rest
outside
of Time.

A foolish belief
That comfort
can be found
holding hands
or resting
in the arms of love,
a soft embrace.

Subscribing
to the notion of
LOVE
as the meaning of life

all the while
aware
of innumerable
examples otherwise
in this
Kali Yuga age.

The End, Again

Shout my truth
Three little words
borne by the winds

Met with silence
harder to take
than any word

dispersed as if
grains of sand
insignificant
and meaningless

The End, Again

Shout my truth
three little words
borne by the winds

Met with silence
hardest to take
than any word

dispersed as if
grains of sand
insignificant
and meaningless

Not With a Bang

Strange
to awaken
not knowing where

Cracked skull
on ice
knocked out
laying on back, outside
unable to move

Quiet acceptance
thinking
this is where
they'll find my body,
frozen
overnight

Lineage
Songs

45

This day
half the world
away
from my start

Waters rush
and flow
along the
river,
along
life

unlike
never ending gaze
forward and
back

Wood frogs bark,
thoughts arise

How to sum
or measure
before it all

drops
away

Dizzying heights,
blazing hells,

mere ripples
in the flow

Echoes of others
noise and
bluster
A life
so far

Fuse
flamed
at both ends
racing to see
where it stops

To measure
meaningless,
the sum's
the same
old or young
a life
with lifetimes left
yet to burn

Martha

For M.W.

Not a month away
from 79th birthday,
gone.

Gone,
Mogen David,
picnic table,
Long Lake water

Gone,
cigarettes,
pizza with SALT

Gone,
pickin' up sticks,
playing cards

Gone,
jean shorts
and
tube top
(well into her matron years)

Gone,
stubborn and
determined.

Gone.
I sit,
lightning bugs
rising from the ground,
memories arise
and float
away on
those wings.

Catching lightning bugs
as a child,
as a father
with my child,
Long Lake water.

Long Lake water
gone,
Grandpa gone,
Dad gone,
parts of Martha
go with each.

Gone,
stuck in apartment,
gone
body in revolt,
Gone.

Gone,
questioning why,
gone.

Gone
waiting
for her first
born grandchild
to be
returned.

Returned,
Martha with
Joe
returned.

Returned,
Martha with her son,
and Joe
returned.

Martha
waving from
the shore,

The waves
beat out

a mournful sound.

Martha is
gone,
returned
to the
shore she
loved.

Martha is returned.

Life and How to Live it

For C.L.

Determined
stubborn
single-minded
set in
her ways

For it to happen,
you MAKE it happen

By sheer
force of will
projecting an
impenetrable
no bullshit zone
like a force-field

Listen,

with me,

closely

ever so faintly
borne by the breeze
you can hear it

just once

more:

"Ach! Bullshit!"

out like
a shot
instantly
when it dared
attempt
to breach
the perimeter

The cord is cut
on your
way in.

The cord is cut
on your
way out.

Faced with
diminishing quality
and machine
dependency

"No. No surgery. No way.
If it's my time, it's my time."

Any surprise
taking control

of that final

choice?

Now the world
is just
a little smaller
worse yet
a little more
tolerant
of
bullshit.

It's up
to
you.

Unintentional Shade

To begin,
the touch
cold, degrees beyond
as if a negative,
a deficit of heat

In Chaos
noticing begins
the bloat
and odor
and the far side
of rigor stiffness
the eyes
the open eyes

as if
though empty
surveying mine
seeing nothing

shrouded, gone beyond
hungry for warmth
and life

as if by taking from mine
it would somehow be permissible

to reignite
his
and begin
again

Fox River Encounter

because of E.H.

Fallen logs, flowing river. Spectral fisher steps out of the mist.

"Son, have a pull from this." A flask. "The fish aren't biting today, but the fishing's good. You don't have a rod. What brings you out here?"

"Forcing myself to take a crash course in learning to relax."

"Well, I'll leave you to it. That's important work."

"Before you go, a question?" A nod. "Why?"

Dissipating into the dark, "because it was the only end," left hanging in the air.

Too Late

Hand on shoulder, breathe in
sit, breathe out
last kiss on forehead, breathe in
sit, breathe out

Cutting the cord
as you come in,
cutting the cord
as you go out

Breath of Life

For C.S.

Wind, breath
air, spirit
soul

Machine breathing
as hammer to
anvil
exhale is impact

Inhale

Impact
of art
on life, in life, as
life,
rising

Release

Rising dance
of art
as expression,
celebration,

exhalation

Inhale

Exhalation
all that departs
pain, inability, fear
wit, compassion

Release

Compassion for life
others and own
safeguarding helper
all

Inhale

All that remains
anger, shock,
absence

Release

Release

Anne

For A.W.
at Dakini Poetics: Experiments of Attention
workshop with Anne Waldman 04/14/2012

Hair black as
Sin
blazing, fierce
intellect
draped in darkness

Flashes of color
punctuating the ongoing
struggle
against the Dark Age

Determined to contribute
Temporary Autonomous Zone
right or wrong
no black or white
soldiering on
lifetimes' commitment

Restoration

Mists shift and switch
through time
Su Tung-p'o scans
shore of West Lake
raises his arms
signals toward the skyscrapers in the distance
banishing them back
as vapors swirl
mountains once again
frame the shoreline
Su, triumphant, blurs
back into haze
and time

Liberation Through Hearing

For P.B.

It's not
hard-headed
differences of opinion
or
awful, time-worn cliches
I still hear, echoing
instead solid directive:
"You already know, do what's right."
followed by laughter

Big, boisterous
laughter

Father's Day

I see my Father's
eyes
when I look back at my own
face

I see my Father's
hands
when my own are
split and scarred

I see my Father's
heart
open and unafraid
when the one I have is shattered
a pale imitation

I hear my Father's
voice
scattering among the leaves
laughing
floating upon the breeze

If only it was just
on Father's Day

Lament

For Dr. J.C.

I.
I sit
and I sit

I sit
in shock,
in anger
I sit

The instruction
is to
breathe

I sit
at the river
as you and I discussed
endlessly
it doesn't matter which,
all rivers are one

II.
I breathe
and I breathe

Unbelieving
I breathe

Dip my hand
in the flow
and breathe

In
exchange
out

In…

III.
I feel
the current
flow

"So we beat on,
boats against the current,
borne back ceaselessly into the past."

Ducklings
push against,
dead branches
drift

I mix
my tears
with the
constant stream

I breathe…

IV.
I rage
against injustice-
of the gift of
time
you gave yourself,
its sudden
revocation
"I just want to write poetry."

The joy with
which you took
to do just that,
making up for
lost
time

I sit
and I breathe
sun reflecting on water

V.
I sit
and I weep
for what else
can a sad poet man
do?

The loss of
poems
unwritten,
conversations
we'll not have

I breathe…

VI.
I think of
the Delta,
your proud home
"I'm so glad you got to go on this adventure."

I sit
as the sun
drops below view
and the
mosquitoes take
their fill

I breathe

In
exchange
and out
 I sit

And

I
breathe…

When I Think of Walt Whitman

*"It's not necessary to refer to him: he's there, always, with
that music, that singing..."*
                                    -C.K. Williams, On Whitman

When the breeze speaks
through the leaves
I think of Walt Whitman
my thoughts turn to
vast expanses, fields to the horizon
lines like the road
that list and meander, winding
mapping the land

When I think of Walt Whitman
enormity looms
the bustle of cities, the babble
of brooks, the braying of
fools, the wise man's lecture
all
thoughts of many, thoughts of one
of parts great and small that
make up the whole

When I think of Walt Whitman
I think of vital spark
When the simple sound and sheer beauty of words
bring me to tears
I think of connection, that pull
between man, woman

present and past
those not yet born, poets to come
all inhabitants of Whitman's America
natural born citizens
bound by no border
sky above, sea below
the grass…

When I think of Walt Whitman
his powerful vision fills my mind, one man
come to embody the concept,
the very definition of poet
his America sung into
being by that singular voice
the rhythm
echoed by many
still sounding
nearing two centuries

When I think of Walt Whitman
I think of
You
and
I
"For every atom belonging to me as good belongs to you"

River
Songs

Inside Information

Shadows crest
waves
Sun's shift
ending

Scent of
open water is
freedom

Sudden downdraft
force of flock
flying overhead

Sheer sound
of wings
beating
against air

Less than an arm span
away,
innumerable wings
working, beating

Orchestration

Wind plays
percussive,
bottle bouncing
down the street

All Rivers Are One

Coincidentally
"Cleansing Day"
reading China's
ancient poets
beside
roar of the river

Poets speak
of Qing Ming Festival,
purification,
of bathing in
the river

As I sit
the river cleanses,
the flow of time
shifts,
leaving me
desirous of
more

Renewal

The scent of water,
lakes, rivers
running
flowing
rushing
baptizing anew

What Did You Do With Yours

The sense of time
along the river

stopped
yet flowing

water rushes
wind blows

every yesterday
up to today

in a flash

trees, buildings
rise, fall

The river
does not
take note
nor
care

Wavecrest

Years drift like tides
ebb and flow
play of light
across the water
color shift blue to green
white, all white

Driftwood

Today was set free
a humble piece of driftwood
incarcerated upon the shelf
a sentence lasting three decades

Launched out upon the river waves
Left to drift and bob
until I lost sight
on out past the horizon

like all those years
spent drying on the shelf

The Quiet

Leaves on the branch
rustling in the breeze
ducks waddling
morning chat
drops of rain
light splash in the river
squirrels scurry down trees
geese landing on water

No one around
to disturb
greeting the sun
as it breaks horizon

Except solitary
writer
starting the day

Progress

Surrounded by
cicadas
chanting
cypress trees

volume greater
than
skyscrapers rising ceaselessly

marking territory
by sound
wave upon wave
erasing
new buildings
striving for sky

Surrounded by
cicadas
chanting
cypress trees
volume greater than
skyscrapers ceaselessly
rising

Marking territory
by sound
wave upon wave
erasing
new buildings
striving for
sky

Currents

<pre>
Sound of river water slows
        the flow of time
                thoughts rise
                        a
                         n
                         d
                          fall
                           rise
                            a
                             n
                             d
                              fall
   sudden slip, clock starts again
                pages drifting by
</pre>

THE ROSETTA
TAZO
green ginger
sound of river water slows   the flow of time
thoughts rise and fall
rise and fall
sudden slip, clock starts again
...pers drifting by

What Will I Do With All That Time?

Bask in sunlight
alongside turtles
aligned in a row
regiments
atop a tree
fallen into
water

Watch dragonflies
dart and hover
black and
iridescent blues

Breathe with river flow
geese landing on water

Fall, Like Rain

Trees torn out
knocked into each other
pulled down
cracked, split open
wildflowers mowed over
leaves of grass ploughed under

Developing along the river
expanding access
concrete and asphalt
old man's tears

River Song

Always seeking
to sit outside of time
gazing beside the river
in thought, realize
the river is
such a place
seasons, years
millennia, more

Within the drift there is no time
water passes like years
always flowing

Look closer
to see the river
is to see
difference
different water
your own and different
older body

River rushing, roaring
high water
rising deeper

revising twists and turns
reclaiming river's edge

rewriting landscape
retaking root lands
snow blowing
landing, flowing
joining the river
sliding into lawns
spraying against risers
slipping over banks
washing, cleansing
beginning anew

Matters not
the season
always onward
lost in the flow
but found
oh, found!

Kisses lit by lunar light
refracted and reflected
off and then
the falling flakes
of snow

Gennett Records
Records
Gennett Records Walk of Fame Celebration
Richmond, IN
October 1st, 2022

All That Remains
Upon viewing the remnants of the Gennett Records facility

Bustling production
vast complex
pianos, phonographs
music first recorded
etched into the grooves

Over time
business lost
Great Depression
forced to close

Complex not maintained
history disregarded
buildings knocked down

One remaining shell
saved before destroyed
sentinel with windows
gone

Wind free to
blow in, around
through

Close your eyes
music in the air
again, floating on
the breeze

Listen.

-Paul Bach

Layout and design by Amanda Graham and
Logan Hendricks

Gennett Records Walk of Fame Celebration
Richmond, IN
October 1st, 2022
All That Remains
upon viewing the remains of the
Gennett Records facility

Bustling production
vast complex
pianos, phonographs
music first recorded
etched into the grooves

Over time
business lost
Great Depression
forced to close

Complex not maintained
history disregarded
buildings knocked down

One remaining shell
saved before destroyed
sentinel with windows gone

Wind free to
blow in, around
through

Close your eyes
music in the air
again, floating on
the breeze

Listen.
-Paul Bach

www.ingramcontent.com/pod-product-compliance
Lightning Source LLC
Chambersburg PA
CBHW071249150726
48001CB00018B/634